Savannah & Grassland Monitors

FROM THE EXPERTS AT
ADVANCED VIVARIUM SYSTEMS®

By Robert George Sprackland, Ph.D., F.L.S., F.Z.S.

Director, The Virtual Museum of Natural History at curator.org.

THE HERPE
Advance
Mission

Library of Congress Cataloging-in-Publication Data

Sprackland, Robert G.
 Savannah and grassland monitors : from the experts at Advanced Vivarium Systems / by Robert George Sprackland.
    p. cm.
Includes bibliographical references (p.   ).
 ISBN 1-882770-53-6 (pbk. : alk paper)
 1. Monitor lizards as pets. 2. Captive lizards. I. Title.
 SF459.L5 S67 2001
 639.3'9596--dc21

                    00-011506

Advanced Vivarium Systems, Inc.
P.O. Box 6050
Mission Viejo, CA 92690 USA
www.avsbooks.com
(877) 4-AVS-BOOK

Printed in Singapore
10 9 8 7 6 5 4 3 2 1

For my friend and colleague,
SEAN McKEOWN,
who has done so much in the
service of herpetoculture.

"Gripping Tail—
Yellow Baboon and
White-Throated
Monitor" (1994
acrylic 30 inches x
20 inches © CP
Brest Van Kempen)

CONTENTS

Preface 6

Introduction 9

Taxonomy 20

Choosing a Specimen 37

Accommodating Lizards 41

Feeding and Nutrition 47

Handling 52

Breeding 54

Veterinary Concerns 58

Life Stages 64

Conclusion 65

Resources 67

Index 70

PREFACE

During the last two decades of the twentieth century, monitor lizards (also called varanids) took the herpetological community by storm. They have served as excellent subjects for ecological, physiological, behavioral, and evolutionary studies, and they make popular exhibits at zoos. Perhaps it is because of this familiarity that they also have become mainstays of the herpetocultural community. Many monitors make excellent captive specimens, being hardy, easy to feed, and long-lived. They recall in us images of dinosaurs and dragons (despite considerable retooling over the past thirty years of what dinosaurs were really like), and many are tractable enough to allow safe handling of even large specimens. The activity and physiology of monitors closely resembles that of many mammals, and their purported intelligence seems on a par with that of birds. All these features have endeared varanids to herpetoculturists. Barring the introduction of inappropriate legislation, varanids are here to stay, whether in our homes, zoos, or schools.

In 1989, the number of species of monitors that had been bred in captivity was tiny. By 1999, a large number of monitor species were being commercially bred to supply the growing pet trade demand. Almost every aspect of biology uses monitors as subject animals in studies, and following this activity have been an extraordinary number of books, articles, specialist study groups, and Web sites devoted to these animals. Hardly a week passes where I do not have Komodo dragons (an Indonesian monitor lizard that may attain a length of 10 feet) enter my living room via the television. In a very real sense they have gone from near obscurity to becoming some of the most intensely studied reptiles. Interest in and appreciation of monitors is, like rock and roll, here to stay.

In choosing a title for this book, I have focused on the habitats of the species included. Thus, savannah (also spelled "savanna") in this sense refers to the savannah habitats of Africa, Asia, and New Guinea. This includes the species referred to as the savannah monitor in the United States (though the same species is known as Bosc's monitor in much of Europe and Africa). The fact that savannah monitors are named after their habitat preference should cause minimal confusion. The value of grouping these particular lizards is not entirely arbitrary because they share similar needs in captivity.

Many people and institutions kindly made specimens and literature available to me for my studies. In reference to this book I extend my thanks to my friends and colleagues for their unselfish help: E.N. Arnold, Michael Balsai, Daniel Bennett, Wolfgang Böhme, Neil Davie, Bernd Eidenmüller, Susan Evans, Rainer Günther, Hans-Georg Horn, Günther Kohler, Bill Love, Colin McCarthy, Sean McKeown, Chip Miller, Barry and Pat Pomfret, Ron Roper, Frank Slavens, Becky Speer, Peter Strimple, Gerry Swan, Michel Thireau, Rainer Thissen, Klaus Wesiack, and Rudolf Wicker. Andy Rowell and Mark Bayless were particularly helpful with information about captive care of savannah monitors. I also thank Mark Bayless for hunting down literature and locality data for African lizards. Institutions that provided access to specimens were: Alexander Koenig Museum (Bonn), California Academy of Sciences (San Francisco), Frankfurt Zoo, Glades Herp (Ft. Meyers), Jungle Larry's (Naples, FL), The Natural History Museum (London), the National Museum of Natural History (Leiden, the Netherlands)The National Museum of Natural History of Paris, The National Museums of Scotland (Edinburgh), The Natural History Museum of Vienna, San Diego Zoo, Senckenberg Museum (Frankfurt), University College London, Woodland Park Zoo (Seattle), the Zoological Museum of Amsterdam, the Zoological Museum at Munich, and the Zoological Museum at Berlin. My editors, Gigi and Philippe de Vosjoli, were extremely helpful and encouraging. I also thank Philippe for his comments and updates on certain aspects of husbandry. As ever, my most special thanks go to my wife, Teri, for her continued support and enthusiasm for my work.

INTRODUCTION

The last decade of the twentieth century saw a remarkable surge of interest in large lizards, including iguanas, tegus, and monitors. Is there a coincidence in the appearance of this interest in and the renewed fascination with dinosaurs? Do we keep such animals because they are our real live link to the types of animals seen in *Jurassic Park?* For that matter, can we deny that the portrayed actions of *Jurassic Park's* velociraptors were inspired by monitor lizards? Though monitors are at best very distant (and not direct) relatives of dinosaurs, they closely fit the image of what we think—or want—a dinosaur to be. Some of the most imposing of these relative giants are found in the savannas of the Southern Hemisphere.

Monitors have roots that extend back at least into the upper Cretaceous Period, over 80 million years ago. Their fossils are found in modern-day Mongolia, Canada, and the northwestern U.S. From the fossil evidence available, it is known that a prehistoric monitor would have been very similar in appearance to one of the living species. In fact, the oldest known fossils represent animals that barely reached 3.2 feet in length, on a par with most of today's species. The distinctions we can detect are minor (though anatomically significant) features, such as the possession of teeth on the palate (living species lack these teeth). Older fossils of lizards very similar to varanids (called varanoids) are known from the early Cretaceous and even the Jurassic Periods. From this and related paleontological data, we can put to rest any notion that monitors are closely related to dinosaurs, as their last common ancestor may well have been in the Triassic Period—meaning that we are about as closely related to dinosaurs as monitors are! Nevertheless, no primate existed to dodge the likes of tyrannosaurus or steal eggs from ceratopsians; but monitors surely did.

As the earth moved into later geological periods and continents moved toward their current positions, monitors, too, migrated over time. North America and Europe were rich in varanids during the Tertiary Period, though by its end some 2 million years ago, all of the American species were extinct. Those in Europe were restricted to the Far East, in Turkey and Arabia, overlapping part of their current westernmost distribution. The modern genus *Varanus* was first positively identified in fossils from Miocene rocks from Kenya, Africa. To my eye, this species is barely discernible from the contemporary Nile monitor *(Varanus niloticus)*. Shortly thereafter, other species appear in the record for India, Indonesia, and Australia. Today, Australia hosts the greatest diversity of monitor species, including the 8-inch dwarf and the 8-foot perentie. Outside Australia, all monitors grow to at least 3 feet in length, excepting a few members of the taxonomically confusing Timor monitor group. These lizards, which rarely exceed 20 inches in total length, are found in New Guinea, Timor, and a few nearby islands.

Anatomy

As a group, monitors are fairly conservative in gross anatomy: they have elongated heads and bodies, long tapering tails, and four limbs, each with five digits. All have ear openings, well-developed eyes with color vision, and moveable eyelids. The tail is muscular and is prehensile to varying degrees. Unlike many other lizards, monitors cannot voluntarily loose a tail and regrow a duplicate later. Most species use the tail as a whip in their own defense. Monitors have elongated throats, which are actually not proportionally larger than in many other lizards. Like other lizards, a monitor's throat is as long as its snout.

All monitors have unusual dorsal scale structure, with a large central scale surrounded by a cluster of smaller scales. Many of these scales contain microscopic sensory organs from which hairlike microstructures protrude. These organs may detect features of touch that help identify members of their own species or help in evaluating foods. For example, I did a study on how monitors decide which food item to consume if given a choice (Sprackland, 1990). The lizards typically rub their snout and lips across offered foods, possibly evaluating texture. (Incidentally, touch is not a single sense, but represents several distinct sensory processes including hot and cold, texture, hardness and softness, pain, and so on.)

Monitors belong to a lineage of lizards that completely lack crests, frills, or other such ornaments. Their nearest relatives are America's venomous beaded lizards, and Borneo's earless "monitor." All these species have long, forked tongues that retract into a sheath in the throat. This organ (like the one found in snakes) is used for detecting taste and smell, and may be indicative of a relationship between monitors and snakes. (It may also represent an unrelated example of convergence, but the jury is still out on this issue.) Monitors are interesting in terms of behavior because of their stereotypical performances. Males may engage in ritual combat, often wrestling from an upright position. Threatened monitors inflate the body and throat, and hiss loudly at perceived enemies. Females of many species lay eggs in concrete-hard termite nests, then return months later to dig the hatchlings out. They show no other vestige of parental care, however.

All monitors have a small opening in the central upper bone of their skulls, a parietal foramen, in which sits a parietal (also called pineal, or third) eye. Most diurnal lizards possess this organ. It is almost a complete eye, with a lens, retinal cells, and a nerve that connects to the brain. However, images do not form in this eye (which is often nearly opaque in adults). Instead, it acts as an ultraviolet (UV) light receptor and seems to control much of a lizard's thermoregulatory behavior. As wavelengths alter, the lizard knows the time of day and whether to bask, forage, or head back to shelter.

All monitors are carnivorous, with most being primarily consumers of arthropods (insects, crabs, spiders) and other small prey items (lizards, eggs, snakes, nestling birds, snails). Only one species is known to actively take fruit as part of its natural diet (the Philippine species *V. olivaceus*), but other species may take some vegetation either by accident or as part of a captive diet. The guts of these predators are thus fairly straight, without the complex folding seen in the intestines of herbivores and omnivores. This feature also allows for rapid digestion and processing of the high-protein diet consumed by monitors.

Yet despite these similarities (and there are many more), monitors are also an incredibly diverse lot. The skull of the smallest species would barely fill the nostril of the largest, with real dimensions going from a mere 8 inches to a bit over 10 feet. The smallest eat tiny insects and other lizards, while the largest take deer and even (very rarely) man. Their coloration goes from solid black to bright green, and chocolate brown to lemon yellow, with patterns that can resemble oriental carpets or be completely one color. A very few species change color depending on temperature or season. They live in trees and deserts, forests and savannahs, beaches and lakes. Colleagues have reported collecting specimens in swimming pools in Africa and Australia. Their nostrils may be tiny pinholes or huge gashlike slits. A few semiaquatic species have valves that close the nostrils when the lizard is submerged. Some have long tails as prehensile as a monkey's, used as a fifth appendage to assist in climbing, while others have flat, crocodile-like tails used in swimming.

So far, I've only enumerated a few external characters. The internal anatomy is equally diverse. The variety of skull and hemipenal structure could fill monographs. To claim that monitors show little diversity is to display ignorance of more than two or three species. What the family Varanidae lacks in numbers (generally held to be forty to fifty species), it makes up for in variety.

Varanid lizards are most numerous in numbers and species in Australia, with variety of species diminishing as one moves west to Africa. They are found in much of the southern hemisphere, including Australia, New Guinea, Indonesia, Asia, and Africa, but they are absent from South America, New Zealand, Tasmania, and Madagascar. Fossil species were once plentiful in northeastern Asia and much of North America. An extinct 24-foot Australian cousin, *V.* (called *Megalania* by many authors) *priscus*, dwarfed today's 10-foot Komodo dragon. Though most living species are desert or semidesert animals, forests and grasslands have their share of these remarkable lizards.

Savannahs and grasslands are similar environments. In fact, savannahs are grasslands that undergo lengthy dry periods, even in nondrought conditions. Such habitats are found on

Notice how this adult male white-throat monitor in a threatening posture is raised on his front limbs and his belly is swollen with air. His display is accompanied by a violent hissing sound.

every continent, save Antarctica, but only those of Africa, Asia, and Australia are inhabited by monitor lizards (though absent from South America, monitors are paralleled there by the distantly related tegus and some iguanas). The species that are encompassed by the grasslands are generally large lizards, ranging in total length from about 3 feet to nearly 9 feet. Not surprisingly, these monitors frequently rank among the top tier of local predators.

Is a Monitor Right for You?

Q: Considering their size and predatory nature, can monitors be considered appropriate pets?

In general, they cannot, though many do become extremely tractable in captivity. Pets are generally conceded to be animals with which humans interact freely and that have some degree of intelligence that allows for considerable reciprocity of inter-

action. While many people have intense feelings for their lizards, it is probably a semantic stretch to think of such lizards as pets.

Nevertheless, tractability makes a desirable trait for an animal to be kept in captivity (and despite protestations to the contrary, even professional animal handlers typically enjoy "tame" specimens), and most monitors fall into the category of tractable. Considering how large many of the species grow, tractability is a decided advantage, at least from the keeper's point of view.

Of course, overall adult size should be a consideration for prospective varanid keepers. Savannah monitors are excellent choices because a really large adult will attain a total length of about 3 feet. Argus monitors may reach 5 feet, though most get to about 3.5 feet and then growth slows considerably. Cape monitors easily approach 6 feet, and records confirm that larger specimens are not rare. Even the most docile lizard can present a keeper with unbelievable complications as it grows past the 3-foot mark.

Monitors are not my recommendation for novices to reptile care. If you are new to reptiles, start with something native, from a habitat similar to where you live. Some exotic species certainly fall into the "novice" category, and include bearded dragons and blue-tongue skinks. Savannah monitors would rank in the intermediate category because of their size and cage and temperature requirements.

If you do decide to get a monitor, have an escape plan in case you don't want it after you see how big it can get. It is completely irresponsible to purchase an animal because it is "cute" and later try to abandon it at a zoo or humane society because—gasp!—it grew. Be informed up front: grassland monitors grow, at least to a yard in length. Zoos rarely take such unwanted animals (they are so common that zoos already have as many as they want, and some zoos lack a reptile house). Humane societies spend a fortune trying to educate people about unwanted pets and won't appreciate your becoming part of the problem. Never release an unwanted exotic pet into your local neighborhood. Initially, it could frighten neighbors, attack (or be attacked by) dogs, or, if it is lucky, survive only until the North American winter kills. (All of these scenarios have occurred.) In 1998, an adult crocodile monitor *(V. salvadorii)* escaped into the San Jose area of California. This is among the most dangerous of monitors and could have caused considerable damage to people, for which the owner would have been legally liable. If you can't make a responsible arrangement for your "pet" should it outgrow your expectations, don't get one in the first place.

Q: Can you get an illness from your monitor?

Yes. Reptiles are susceptible to infection by many bacteria that can also affect humans, including salmonella and strains of pneumonia. If you keep terraria reasonably clean and take care to carefully wash your hands after every time you handle a lizard or something in its cage, you minimize the risk of contracting such an infection. In fact, unless you are incredibly careless, it is very unlikely you will catch something from a reptile.

Q: How long do monitors live?

Monitors are probably much longer-lived than we know at this time. Certainly, savannah and white-throat monitors have been kept in captivity in excess of twelve years, but their size in nature suggests that they may live closer to thirty to fifty years in

Savannah monitors are often described as having the potential for being "dog tame." This specimen attracted the attention of a photographer while it was walking with its owner.

the wild. Argus monitors have also been kept for about a decade, but it is likely they live at least fifteen years. This is still an area about which we know far too little. In short, though, plan that a monitor will be part of your household for a period of time similar to a typical dog's life span.

Q: Do monitors smell?

(Is there an experienced keeper who isn't smiling?) In fact, the lizards have very little odor, but their feces and ruined food can be downright foul. Keeping the smell under control requires hygiene, frequent replacement of substrate, and prompt removal of messes and uneaten food. Many monitors give their water bowl double duty as swimming pool and toilet, so it, too, must be cleaned daily to keep odors at bay. There is a wonderful terrarium deodorizer product available called Bio-Fresh.

As long as I'm treading on the responsibility issue, there are a few other responsibilities that you as an owner of any reptile should be prepared to shoulder:

- Excepting some snakes, reptiles require food much more frequently than once a month, so be prepared to feed them as they need.
- Never, ever, under any circumstances use a reptile to scare or surprise someone! It is not only grossly irresponsible to your friend but it reinforces the unpleasant image many people still have toward reptiles.
- Do not keep more animals than you can properly care for.
- Be sure to wash your hands thoroughly with soap (preferably antibacterial soap) and hot water after handling your animals and cage props. This reduces the likelihood of you or your other housemates contracting a disease.

Savannah and Cape monitors are being successfully kept in captivity all over the world. Some keepers provide spacious indoor concrete enclosures. Others use off-the-shelf aquariums and accessories. Others house their charges outdoors. The point here is that herpetoculture is a bit like medicine, a blend of science, art, and practice. There is no general formula for successful herpetoculture, though some guidelines give your animals a better chance at survival than others. Good hygiene, appropriate diet and temperature regimes, and regular careful observations of your charges are the essentials of good herpetoculture. The rest is highly individualized.

There can be little doubt that the grassland monitors include the most widely sought species by novice varanid keepers. They generally grow to manageable size, feed on a wide variety of foods, and have peaceful temperaments. Many make exceptionally good exhibition animals, both for caged exhibits and for live-animal demonstrations. Add to this their general availability and modest cost, and the reasons for their popularity are clear. To this list of pluses must be added the increased

frequency of captive breeding, making undamaged, nonwild specimens more common in the market. In my opinion, however, the only nongrassland species that would be good for novice monitor keepers is Duméril's monitor from Southeast Asia. And this would still be an intermediate animal in the overall selection of reptiles coupled with your experience.

Legal Issues

Be advised that monitors are not for everyone. Savannah species grow fairly large, need roomy quarters, and make creative messes. They cost time, money, and effort to care for properly. A bite from a large monitor can be a serious problem, possibly requiring stitches or worse. Be sure to check your local laws, because some municipalities ban certain animals or species that grow over a certain size. True, people do still keep ferrets in California (where it is illegal) and people do keep large monitors and snakes in San Francisco (also illegal), but in violating such laws you may bring community wrath upon those of us who practice legal and responsible herpetoculture. Do your homework and check on all implications of your decision to own monitors before taking the plunge.

Monitors are rare or threatened in many places. Though people may revere or ignore them in some locations, most humans see monitors as merely another source of income. The primary consumption of monitors is the international leather trade. Designer fashion commands huge prices for monitor (sometimes labeled simply "lizard") products. Without doubt, thousands of times more monitors fall prey to the leather industry than to the live animal trade. Loss of habitat and use for foods and medicines (of dubious efficacy) also take an incredible toll on these animals. Many people believe that once an animal is listed by the Convention on International Trade in Endangered Species of Wild Fauna and Flora (CITES) or the Endangered Species Act it is somehow protected. Quite the contrary, such listing merely regulates international trade, while continued exploitation often continues in the home country. It is also true that some populations face depredation by overzealous collectors for the pet trade, and such exploitation is a bane to herpetoculture. Suggestions to impose collecting quotas meet with varying degrees of success (as do attempts to enforce such laws). Many other animals are collected by people who see their animals as a cash resource that must be self-regulated, lest they face going out of business. Such entrepreneurs, however, are few and far between, which is yet another strong case for buying captive-bred animals. But for animals that do arrive safely from abroad, and especially those that are bred to supply offspring for the trade, it is the herpetoculturist's responsibility to provide the very best of care possible. To paraphrase Star Wars' Yoda: Do it right, or do it not!

TAXONOMY

Breeding, housing, and environmental considerations for any captive species have their foundation in taxonomy. Taxonomy is the branch of biology that deals with the naming and classification of species. To have a name for an organism is to have a sort of call number that facilitates finding information about that species, or, if such data are lacking, about similar closely related species. While captive reproduction has been documented between species and even genera, such successful hybrids are usually the result of careful planning by the breeders. Animals rarely attempt to breed outside their own species, yet the incredible range of variation exhibited by creatures with almost limitless genetic diversity makes determination of species difficult in many cases. However arcane or distasteful it may seem to some keepers, having access to solid taxonomic information is essential to the proper breeding of any organism, especially if genetic integrity is a goal of such breeding.

Despite taxonomy's rather low esteem in the eyes of many professional and amateur biologists, it is a complex and discriminating discipline with important implications for anyone contemplating responsible captive breeding (let alone any other facet of zoology). However, the practice of taxonomy and the rules governing the application and use of names have been subject to considerable vacillation and controversy, with the result that the status of many monitor species is subject to question. Even practicing taxonomists are besieged with new methods of interpretation that, at first appearance, seem to fly in the face of reason.

Monitor lizards are still considered to be members of the class Reptilia. They are also lizards in the superfamily Varanoidea (also called Platynota) in the family Varanidae. Though a few workers consider the Varanidae to be made up of two genera of living lizards, *Lanthanotus* and *Varanus*, I consider the family to be represented solely by the latter. The sole genus of living monitors includes about forty recognized species of lizards that range in size from 8 inches to over 10 feet.

The story of how the name *monitor* was applied to these lizards is interesting. Albertus Seba, an eighteenth-century apothecary and naturalist, used the term *sauvegarde* (meaning *safeguard*) in referring to tegus in his collection (tegus are South American lizards that resemble monitors but are only distantly related to them). He relates a story in which they whistled at the approach of caimans, warning men to safety (Anderson, 1898 and Sprackland, 1992). It is not unreasonable to suppose that the whistling sound was really the hissing varanids make when under threat, and that early observers mistook this sound as a personal warning to them! In time, this "warning" function became Latinized *(monitor)* and gave us our current vernacular name for the group.

There has been considerable debate over the specification and number of subgenera to be used, with more recent studies coming ever closer in agreement. The subgenus name follows the genus name in parentheses: for example, the savannah monitor is currently classified as *V. (Polydaedalus) exanthemati-cus*. A subgenus is a species group that shares certain traits in common that are not shared with other groups. A subgenus is typically designated within an otherwise uniform genus to show the lines of relatedness among the different species. Sometimes a subgenus is designated for a well-known species group so that the genus name—the call number of the biological library's literature—doesn't change. Biologists disagree about what constitutes a change in genus names. So far, one of the few things all varanid biologists have agreed upon is the retention of the single widespread genus name, *Varanus*.

Nevertheless, the status of subgenera, particularly for Australian species, is in enough of a state of flux that I shall not use subgenera in the following discussions. Persons enthralled by the variation in subgeneric allotments are directed to the publications of Mertens (1942), Holmes et al. (1976), and King and King (1975); for a counterview, see Sprackland (1991). For whatever it is worth, taxonomic questions have recently become more prominent in both academic and private sectors, with both considerable revision and controversy. The taxono-

my I employ herein is pretty much the conservative line based on my own studies.

The varanid species that inhabit grasslands are found across the range of the genus, including most of Africa, India, Burma (Myanmar), Vietnam, China, Malaysia, Indonesia, and New Guinea. Many of these animals live in variable environments with both hot dry seasons and cool wet ones. Daily temperatures may be fairly steady during the hottest parts of the year, with considerable variation during the spring and fall. For many of these animals, the monsoons are a vital part of the annual cycle, heralding a period of water and food abundance, followed by periods of active mating. Of the species considered in this book, all but one are largely tropical (i.e., residents of areas close to the equator). The exception (and most cold tolerant) is the white-throat monitor, found to the southern tip of Africa.

The African Species

The most familiar terrarium monitor is probably the savannah monitor, also known as Bosc's monitor. Until the 1990s, the savannah monitor was the species of *Varanus* illustrated in herpetology books (Schmidt and Inger, 1957; Pope, 1955). It has

long been one of the three most highly collected varanid species (along with Nile and water monitors) for the pet trade. Alas, these three species also represent the varanids most highly exploited for their fine leather skin. For many years the similar white-throat monitor was considered a subspecies, but recognition of the two as distinct began with Bill Branch's study of hemipenal structure (Branch, 1982). The moderate size and calm temperament have contributed to the long-term popularity of this species. (A note on the other species I just mentioned: Nile monitors are known for their nastiness and difficulty in keeping young specimens alive, while young water monitors are also difficult to get to feed properly. Both species reach adult sizes in excess of 6 feet and are especially not recommended for novices. The Nile is primarily a forest or desert dweller and is not a subject for this book.)

Savannah monitors (V. exanthematicus) are inhabitants of sub-Saharan and northeastern Africa, ranging from Senegal in the west through Sudan and Egypt in the east. There is a gap of some two hundred to three hundred miles in central Africa that apparently divides the species' range in two sections. Savannah

Varanus p. panoptes, the Australian subspecies.

A nice specimen of an adult male white-throat monitor *(V. albigularis),* showing how big a still-growing lizard can get.

monitors are lowland species found below 1,000 feet, and though they may approach deserts, they are restricted by proximity to river courses. During part of the year they dwell near water, while much of the time they live in very arid habitats. Adults tend to be a drab gray with prominent black circles on the back, but the ground color may range toward rusty (central Africa) or almost tan (Sudan). They are further easily recognized in having an oval nostril that sits about midway between the tip of the snout and the eye, having a light gray or cream-colored throat (never black), and in having a tail that is only a little longer than the snout-vent length. Savannah monitors are medium-sized lizards, reaching an adult length of 36-40 inches.

The scales of savannah monitors are round or slightly oval, and large enough to be conspicuous without magnification. These scales give the lizards a durable, thick, waterproof skin, precisely the features that make them so popular as a source of leather.

The head of a savannah monitor is a boxlike structure, neither elongated nor elegant as that seen in most varanids. This boxiness is notable even in hatchlings barely the length of an adult human's finger (in contrast, white-throat monitors have flatter heads until they get to subadult stage). If tree monitors resemble herons and Argus monitors recall hawks, then savannah monitors are the parrots of the monitor group. This boxy

A light phase of white-throat monitor *(V. albigularis)* originally from Mozambique.

A dark phase of white-throat monitor *(V. albigularis)* originally from East Africa.

head belies very strong crushing jaws that can easily break clam and snail shells, part of the seasonal diet in the wild.

At this time, the white-throat monitor *(V. albigularis)* is achieving popularity to rival that of the savannah. The white-throat is also known by a variety of common names including leguaan, Cape monitor, and black-throat monitor. There have been several subspecies attributed to *V. albigularis,* but studies I am publishing with Mark Bayless have failed to establish justification for subspecies. The name *"albigularis"* literally translates from Latin to "white throat," but the species is actually characterized (at least in young specimens) by a black throat. In some individuals the black becomes a gray in adults. I assume that

Underside of subadult white-throat monitor. By adulthood, the characteristic dark throat (which is nearly universal in young) has all but faded away.

describer François Daudin was actually referring to the light coloring of the lips and chin of his holotype. No matter, "white-throat" has stuck, and has led to considerable confusion among specialists and amateurs alike. The white-throat monitor has a longer tail than the savannah monitor has, and the slitlike nostril is so near the eye that it appears to be in contact with it. The white-throat monitor is slimmer in build than the savannah monitor and grows much larger, approaching 6 feet in total length.

White-throat monitors are broadly distributed across Africa, from the horn of Somalia in eastern Africa south to South Africa, and north on the west to Angola. They are rare at altitudes above 1,800 feet, but their distribution is contiguous through mountain passes through the entire range. They prefer more reliable water sources than do savannah monitors and are more apt to be found in jungle areas than are other similar species. The considerable literature recognizing subspecies is generally based on examination of limited or immature specimens. The so-called "ionidesi" phase (as *V. albigularis ionidesi*) was described from juveniles collected in Tanzania. However, I have examined nearly identical specimens from parts of South Africa and central Angola. The lack of true geographic limits to subspecies patterns was in large part responsible for the decision that Mark Bayless and I made to eliminate all the subspecies. At this time, we recognize only *V. albigularis*.

Savannah and white-throat monitors are superficially similar in appearance, especially between adults. Adults of both savannah and white-throat monitors have high, blunt snouts, but juveniles of white-throat monitors have flatter, more "typical" varanid-shaped snouts. They also have similar ecologies, which probably accounts for the considerable convergence in morphologies. Nevertheless, the two species are easily distinguished in the following table.

Savannah Monitor	White-Throat Monitor
Body gray or dark tan with black-ringed light spots on the back	Body dark brown or dark gray, with variable dorsal pattern
Nostril about midway between the eye and the tip of the snout	Nostril very close to eye, almost inside orbital ring of scales
Body without bands	Body usually has at least faint bands
Seven to eight scales between eye and ear	Fourteen or more scales between eye and ear
Neck scales much larger than body scales and are round	Neck scales slightly larger than body scales and are usually oval
Throat light gray or cream, never black	Throat with a dark, often black, center
Tail little more than snout-vent length	Tail much longer than snout-vent length
Maximum total length about 3 feet, 3 inches	Maximum total length in excess of 6 feet, 6 inches

There are also numerous differences between savannah and white-throat monitors, particularly in regards to hemipenal structure (Branch, 1982; Böhme, 1989) and cranial osteology (Bayless and Sprackland, 2000). Though they have some ecological overlap, white-throat monitors are more apt to climb or take to water than are savannahs. A final feature that can distinguish older specimens of these similar species is that the teeth of white-throat monitors often become blunted, molarlike structures, presumably an adaptation to crushing clams, snails, and the bones of larger vertebrate prey. In contrast, the teeth of savannah monitors tend to remain pointed.

Savannah monitors frequent the broad grasslands of central Africa. These habitats are seasonally very dry or subject to intense seasonal rains. Savannah monitors are absent from deserts and forests, though they may dwell near the borders of such habitats. There is a huge distributional gap that spans most of Chad and divides the species into two large populations. The

An interesting yellowish color phase of the savannah monitor. This is a juvenile the author photographed through the courtesy of "Dances with Snakes" pet shop in San Jose, Calif.

eastern population ranges from Uganda and southern Sudan north to central Sudan and extreme western Ethiopia.

The southeastern population is distinguished by a mustard-yellow dorsal color, pink tongue, smaller neck scales, unspotted belly, and paired nasal bones. Recognition of this species was widespread among field workers (Schmidt, 1919) until Robert Mertens synonymized it with *V. exanthematicus* in 1942. Mertens also caused considerable taxonomic confusion by placing all white-throat monitors as subspecies of *V. exanthematicus*. In a separate paper, Bayless and Sprackland (2000) argue for recognition of the southeastern population of monitors as *V. ocellatus,* a name proposed by Carl Heyden in 1830.

Savannah monitors are typically some shade of gray, with light-ringed ocelli (eyelike spots with dark centers) arranged symmetrically on the back. The lower flanks have dark bars, and young animals tend to have a dark postocular streak, which fades in most adults. The nuchal (top of neck) scales are considerably larger than the dorsal scales and tend to be round in shape. Despite being old and familiar species, there has been little research into any aspect of the biology of savannah monitors. Daniel Bennett (Bennett, 1998) has done considerable fieldwork and published several important contributions. Mark Bayless has worked almost exclusively with this animal in captivity, with contributions regarding husbandry and reproduc-

tion (Bayless and Reynolds, 1992). Pete Strimple has written excellent overviews of the savannah/white-throat group (1988–1989).

The Cape (white-throat) monitor is a widespread species with an African distribution second only to that of the Nile monitor. Not surprising in such a dispersed species, there is a considerable variety of patterns found in white-throats. Bayless and Sprackland (2000) have documented that these patterns are not indicative of subspecies because populations are contiguous across Africa. Instead, there is a direct correlation between pattern and color with habitat and rainfall. Given any feature we studied, from scale size to pattern style, there is continuous clinal variation, which means the two distant ends of a range may be very similar, while the central region differs markedly from both. Such indicators point toward environmental, not genetic, causes for observable variation.

White-throat monitors are among the half-dozen or so best-studied varanids in terms of overall research activity (ecology, anatomy, physiology, distribution, husbandry, and reproduction) with much of the leading edge work coming from the San Diego Zoo's Center for Research on Endangered Species. Consequently, herpetoculturists may draw on considerable recent research to enhance their success in keeping this species.

It is possible that a population of monitors resembling savannah monitors deserves recognition at the species level. This is an example of that species *(V. ocellatus)* from Sudan.

For examples of this work, see Alberts (1994), Lemm (1998), Phillips and Millar (1998), and Phillips and Packard (1994).

India has a savannah dweller, the gold monitor *(V. flavescens)*, which has habits similar to those of the white-throat monitor. *Varanus flavescens* is very similar to both savannah and white-throat monitors in appearance (though different in color), which had resulted in it being classified in a subgenus with those species until recently. This Asian species is actually much more closely related to the Bengal and Indian monitors.

At present, Indian monitors are legally considered to be subspecies of Bengal monitors. This is important for herpetoculturists to understand because it means that under the law, Indian monitors are still considered Appendix I animals under CITES and the Endangered Species Act.

The Asian Species

Five Asian taxa qualify as savannah dwellers and include the Argus, Bengal, Indian, and gold monitors and the famous Komodo dragon. The Argus monitor *(V. panoptes)* has rapidly become a mainstay of the herpetocultural market and though pricier than the African species, is almost as frequently encountered in the more diverse reptile specialty shops. The considerable success in captive breeding of this species assures it will remain a staple in the reptile trade.

A colorful phase of the white-throat monitor (head and tongue shot). Though this phase was long given subspecies recognition, it is not restricted in range in accord with the application of subspecies names.

The endangered and beautiful yellow monitor, *V. flavescens*. Though it resembles the savannah monitor, it is actually much more closely related to the Indian and Bengal monitors.

Argus monitors are indigenous to southern lowland New Guinea, and most specimens are obtained from the Indonesian half of that island, Irian Jaya. The subspecies most commonly available *(V. panoptes horni)* is named for German varanid researcher Hans-Georg Horn and is distinguished from the similar Australian taxon primarily in having a distinct pattern of large dark spots on the belly and throat. In addition, the Australian subspecies are desert and peripheral grassland species, while the Argus monitor is a true grassland resident.

Unlike most of the other grassland monitors, Argus monitors are brilliantly colored. The dorsal background is a shade of honey or chocolate brown. The back is covered with alternating rows of small black and yellow spots. There are two distinct, dark streaks on the face, one a pre-/postocular stripe, the other below that and bordering the upper lips. The spots are slightly larger on the tail, where they form rings. The last one-fifth to

one-third of the tail is solid yellow. The top of the head is dark. The lower surfaces are cream to bright yellow, with large dark spots. The intense pattern of light and dark provides excellent camouflage in the wild. The name "Argus" comes from the many eyelike spots ("*panoptes*" means "all eyes") on the back, for Argus was a deity with a thousand eyes from Greek mythology.

Argus monitors are quickly becoming one of the most popular reptiles available today. Though they can become quite large—growing to about 5 feet—they are frequently docile enough to allow casual handling. They are voracious and ready feeders, and they are more active than many of their relatives. Many people are now breeding Argus monitors, so availability is high, and captive-hatched juveniles are among the prettiest of lizards.

Like other members of the Gould's monitor species group, Argus monitors have the interesting ability to tripod. Lizards rear up, straight-backed, and balance on their hind limbs and tail. In this stance they closely resemble African meerkats as they periscope above the tall grass. Young specimens may also run in a nearly upright posture (adults may attempt this, but their posture is almost always far less than upright).

Though this species was not named until 1980, considerable field studies have been conducted on the Australian subspecies, *V. panoptes panoptes.* However, it wasn't until Shine (1986) published his ecological notes on four sympatric (living in the same area) monitor species that many researchers accepted *V. panoptes* as actually being distinct from the more familiar Gould's monitor, *V. gouldii*. It has subsequently been learned that these two closely related and similar species have considerably different ecologies.

The reptile market has witnessed a large influx of the Australian members of the species complex known broadly as Gould's monitors (named for noted nineteenth-century ornithologist John Gould, the "English Audubon"). Many of these lizards are very similar to New Guinea's Argus monitor, but the Australians lack large black ventral (belly) spots. Some of these animals do inhabit grasslands, so their care would be the same as for the New Guinea form.

The remaining grassland species are listed on Appendix I of CITES, which means acquisition for commercial purposes is extremely limited (the only other Appendix I monitors are the Philippine's Gray's monitor and the wide-ranging desert monitor). The Indian and Bengal monitors have long been considered subspecies of *V. bengalensis*, an opinion maintained by Walter Auffenberg (1994) based on ecological and morphological studies. More recent work by German herpetologists Wolfgang Böhme and Thomas Ziegler (1997) have elevated the subspecies, a view I endorse. Thus, we now consider the widespread and spotted Bengal monitor as *V. bengalensis*, and the dusky, yellowish Indian monitor, *V. nebulosus*. These very similar taxa may be distinguished as shown in the following table.

Both Indian and Bengal monitors may resemble Argus

Indian Monitor (V. nebulosus)	Bengal Monitor (V. bengalensis)
Supraocular scales enlarged.	Supraoculars subequal in size to nearby scales.
Body with distinct, if faint, dark bands.	Body with light bands in young; adults dusky.

monitors, particularly when young, but differ in having lighter heads, broader snouts, dark tails without a light tip, and nostrils located about midway between the eye and snout tip (in Argus

Varanus bengalensis, the Bengal monitor, may reach a length of 6 feet. This photo was taken at the Vienna Zoo.

monitors the nostril is quite near the snout tip).

Varanus bengalensis is the western member of this group, found from Pakistan south to southern India, Sri Lanka, the Himalayan foothills, and southern China, to eastern and southern Burma (Myanmar). *Varanus nebulosus* ranges from central Burma, Thailand, and Vietnam east to western Borneo and Java.

Indian monitors *(V. nebulosus)* were once the most commonly available species in the U.S. pet trade. (Old-timers will appreciate my memory of purchasing a young specimen in 1969 for $12.50—retail!) They are still more likely to be encountered in the U.S. than Bengal monitors are, and captive breeding, though spotty, is increasing.

Indian monitors are wonderful lizards that are hardy and well dispositioned in captivity. Juveniles are positively birdlike in habits, with long pointed snouts and jerky head movements. They are also predominantly pale yellow, especially on the head, until they reach a total length of about 20 inches. The name *nebulosus* means cloudy and refers to the irregular pattern on the back. While most monitors have spots that form distinct bands and symmetrical patterns, this is not so for

Indian monitors. As they grow, they become more tan than yellow, and wild, dust-covered specimens may be khaki.

Indian monitors are among the most diverse in habits of all varanids. They will readily climb, run, dig, or swim. They excavate long burrows in which they escape the heat of the midday. Their claws are strong enough to rip termite nests apart to lay their eggs inside. Though juveniles and young lizards (up to 15 inches total) tend to remain skittish, older lizards become quite mellow and handleable. If it weren't for the (present) limited availability and high prices associated with Indian monitors, they would doubtless be more popular in herpetocultural circles.

Gold monitors *(V. flavescens)* are protected under CITES Appendix I and are rarely encountered in zoos and thus rarely become available to private keepers. They are beautiful animals, similar in appearance to savannah monitors, but brightly marked with yellow and red. The nostril is more anterior than in Indian and Bengal monitors, the pattern of light spots forming bands is retained in adults, and the supraoculars are about the same size as surrounding scales.

Komodo dragons are extremely well-studied lizards

Varanus flavescens, the Indian gold monitor, is an endangered species rarely found on dealer lists or in zoos. It is very similar in appearance to savannah and white-throat monitors.

The famous Komodo monitor, *V. komodoensis* qualifies as a savannah resident, but is neither available in the trade nor appropriate for private facilities.

(Auffenberg, 1981; Pfeiffer, 1964) that have been successfully bred in zoos during the late 1990s. However, it is unlikely that this species will be encountered outside the zoo world for some time.

CHOOSING A SPECIMEN

Deciding to keep a varanid lizard in captivity involves making a considerable commitment in time, space, and money. No animal, pet or otherwise, should be obtained on a whim or as a casual choice. Monitors grow large enough that the keeper must exercise caution when handling and caging specimens. Consider that bigger lizards (even the smallest of our grassland species, the savannah monitor, reaches 3 feet in length) require more food, make bigger messes that produce greater odors, and need more space than smaller lizards. Teeth and claws are large enough to produce serious injuries. The cost of utilities to heat and light large cages is a factor to consider. You must also be responsible enough to consider an exit strategy, so that if a big lizard turns out to be more than you care to cope with, you have a good home lined up for it. Zoos are not usually appreciative of receiving overgrown and unwanted "pets," and many downright refuse them. This book points out some of the potential pitfalls in store for keepers of large lizards, and there are other guides with additional information (de Vosjoli, 1999; Balsai, 1992; Bennett, 1998; Sprackland, 1992).

There are two primary ways to obtain a monitor, either in person at a shop or by mail order. There are advantages to both approaches, though I advise novice keepers to decide with care.

Pet Shop

A visit to a pet shop (or a reptile show) gives you the chance to see the lizard before paying for it and allows you a firsthand inspection to assure the health of your intended purchase. If you have some experience as a herpetoculturist, this is often the preferred way to go. My one caveat about buying from a pet shop is restricted to my concerns for novice reptile keepers: while many shops have adequately knowledgeable staff, the vast majority of pet shop workers are not informed enough to help people with limited experience. Many of us old-timers have witnessed the sad performance of untrained store workers advising lizard purchasers to feed a monitor a mouse once a month or some lettuce, or telling buyers that a single 25-watt bulb will provide enough heat and light for a 2-foot monitor. This goes for both reptile specialty stores and neighborhood shops. Many people are working to improve this situation. For example, the Northern Ohio Association of Herpetology has held seminars for pet shop workers, while the Pet Industry Joint Advisory Council provides reptile handler certification courses.

What this all means is that the real responsibility for making a sound choice at a pet shop resides with you, the purchaser. There are several things to look for when buying a monitor. First is the "gestalt" appearance of the lizard—is it robust, active, and alert? A robust lizard is neither emaciated nor obese. Check the hip area of a thin lizard. The hip bones should not be visible as bony humps. Healthy monitors have stout, muscular tails with a modest amount of stored fat, obscuring any trace of the underlying bones. In lizards where bones are visible, special care is required to bring the animal back to health. Leave such lizards to experts and veterinarians. At the other extreme are obese lizards—usually older specimens that have been traded in for another animal. Obesity is the product of overfeeding, and may be accompanied by liver, kidney, or circulatory distress. The relatively slow rate of reptilian physiology may allow an obese animal to last a long time before serious illness manifests itself.

Because monitors are active predatory foragers, a healthy lizard should be expected to be moving, or at least ready to move if touched or picked up. True, monitors may become tame in captivity, but young or freshly imported lizards should still exhibit a certain degree of wariness. Lizards that don't respond to handling may be cold, underfed, or ill. When walking, a monitor holds its belly off the ground; if the animal drags its belly, there may well be a physical problem. Check the armpits, groin, ears, and neck folds for signs of external parasites, such as mites and ticks. Ticks are also commonly found in and near the cloaca of wild-caught specimens. Parasites often induce diseases, and lethargy is a common symptom of such infestations.

Eyes should be clear and shouldn't have tearlike fluids. Likewise, nostrils should be clean and free of any debris. Clogged nostrils are often signs of respiratory distress or pneumonia, conditions notoriously difficult and costly to treat. When examining the mouth, the teeth should be visible, and the oral tissues free of waxy or slimy masses. Yellowish material is symptomatic of mouth-rot, an extremely contagious and difficult to treat reptilian malady.

While it is possible to obtain a healthy specimen from a crowded terrarium, I would frown upon doing so unless you had experience enough to be reasonably sure the lizard was healthy. There is no sight more demeaning to herpetoculture that a terrarium overstocked with specimens, crawling and messing on top of each other. The excuse that it is merely a temporary condition is nonetheless also a mere excuse. Remember that you are buying a living creature, subject to similar needs as yourself for hygiene, decent food, and space (yes, that includes psychological space; varanids are definitely territorial). If the dealer is so slovenly as to stack animals like cards, my best advice is *caveat emptor et ambula:* buyer beware and keep walking.

Dealers

Buying through a specialty dealer can simplify lizard acquisition, especially if you order through a well-known and respected dealer. Few fly-by-night operators last more than a few years in the business because word of mouth (and, frequently, legal implications) of their dealings eventually catch up with them. Experienced dealers made their reputations by providing good animals to zoos, breeders, and hundreds of satisfied customers. They also have excellent ties to captive breeders, and the number one choice for a new animal is a captive-bred one. Finding a good dealer isn't too difficult. Most companies run ads in the herpetocultural magazines. Scan current issues and those from a few years ago. If an ad is found in both, you know the dealer has been around for a while. Ask herpetoculturists or zookeepers, who generally have one or two sources that can be trusted to provide quality animals.

A captive-raised, tame hypomelanistic savannah monitor, owned by Reptile Haven in Oceanside, Calif.

Health

Even the most reputable supplier may provide an animal that has a hidden health problem. Remember that you are purchasing a living creature, subject to innumerable sources of potential harm and illness, and no one can reasonably guarantee the long-term health or life span of an animal. The prudent purchaser will put any new animal in quarantine away from other animals and observe the specimen carefully for a minimum of thirty days before placing it near the regular collection. Quarantine should entail an easy-to-clean no-frills terrarium in a quiet area. This allows the animal to gradually adjust to your activity with reduced opportunities for trauma. A lizard should always have access to clean water and both hot and cool areas so it can escape the heat.

Considering the cost in time and money that a monitor entails, it's a good idea to take your acquisition to a competent reptile veterinarian for a checkup. Seek the veterinarian carefully, as reptile specialists are few in number and reptiles respond very poorly, even fatally, to dog- and cat-based medical approaches. You want the veterinarian to check stool samples for signs of internal parasites and provide blood tests that may reveal other potential pathogens.

ACCOMMODATING LIZARDS

I f you are planning to keep medium to large monitor lizards, plan to provide large terraria. Wild monitors are wide-ranging, foraging predators that normally cover several acres of ground per day. Terrarium life will not, and can not, compensate for the lack of natural space, but you can provide adequate space to allow the lizard to have a comfortable life. Small monitors can be safely housed in readily available glass terraria (Plexiglas works, too, from a safety standpoint, but monitors usually claw the material into unsightly opacity.) that include securely fitting lids. As a rule of thumb, figure that a terrarium should be two times as long as the lizard to be housed, and add another lizard length for each additional resident.

As lizards grow, they require larger terraria, and these must often be custom-built. Herpetoculturists with carpentry skills can assemble decent cages, and several companies make custom units. Fortunately, the custom cage builders are often familiar with the animals their cages will house, so it is unlikely that you will wind up with a product that is too weak or dangerous to house large lizards.

The question of how big a terrarium you need is a serious one. Certainly, no varanid will suffer from too much room. In nature, savannah-dwelling monitors forage widely over great distances, such that converting an entire suburban home into a terrarium would fall far short of replicating natural conditions. The upside to terraria, however, is that the keeper obviates the need for foraging by providing food and potential mates to the animals. Captive wild-caught varanids quickly adjust to this situation, while captive-bred specimens have less of an adjustment to make (another big plus for captive-bred stock).

An adult (3-foot) savannah monitor requires a 6-foot x 2-

Arguably the longest monitor is a New Guinea tree dweller. Known as the crocodile monitor *(V. salvadorii)*, it has long, flattened teeth that more closely resemble a shark's than it does other monitors' teeth and may inflict a serious bite. This specimen is feeding on a large adult rat.

foot terrarium as a minimum. A pair of such monitors should have a wider cage (at least 3 feet wide). Commercially available terraria include those with sliding glass fronts (e.g., from Bush Herpetoculture and Vision Herpetoculture), and some large aquaria (75 gallons or larger) are also adequate for lizards this size. Remember that lizards need room to move and exercise, lest they become obese. Argus monitors of similar size will need even more room—say 8 feet x 3 feet or more—because of their greater activity.

Adults of larger monitor species almost always require custom-built terraria because there is too small a market for regular suppliers to manufacture such huge enclosures. Welded wire or, better yet, plastic-coated wire walk-in aviaries (birdcages) are good alternatives, particularly in places where cages may safely be kept outdoors. Large monitors need at least 8 feet x 7 feet of floor space, and 8 feet of vertical space (especially white-throats, which are climbers).

Of the grassland monitors, the Argus is perhaps the most active species and the taxon that will require the roomiest quarters. However, terrarium accommodations for all species are fairly similar. These animals are climbers as young lizards, becoming largely terrestrial as adults. Small monitors may climb trees to avoid predation by a host of species, including larger specimens of their own kind. Trees also offer innumerable good basking sites and many sources of invertebrate foods, from locusts to snails. Consider using a taller-than-long cage for housing young monitors, and switching to a longer-than-tall cage for adults.

Monitors may rival snakes as escape artists because they are strong and active when it comes to finding a way out of a cage. Be sure vivaria have well-fitted doors or tops and that escape is unlikely. It is also prudent to have locks on cages with larger lizards, not so much to keep lizards in but unauthorized fingers out! If you have young children in the house, this is an important precaution.

All monitors should be provided with a water dish large enough to immerse the lizard. While lizards require clean water at all times, hygiene is difficult with creatures that simultaneously use their water container as drinking fountain, swimming pool, and toilet. Frequent cleaning is part of the chore of monitor husbandry, and is especially important when it involves the water supply. Small to medium lizards (6–18 inches) may use plastic shoeboxes as water bowls. Larger specimens may require a plastic or ceramic tub.

Heat is essential to keeping varanids healthy. Heat may be provided by lamps, undercage heat pads and strips, room heating, direct sunlight, or a combination of these. I do not advocate heat rocks for the reason that monitors judge heat by the parietal eye, on top of the head. It is a common problem of heat rocks that animals will sit on them and literally burn, requiring veterinary attention or leading to death. Spotlights in ceramic bases are highly recommended heat sources, and these should be suspended over one end of the terrarium, and well away from access by the lizards. Though heat is essential, so is light, so even if you use a heat lamp, be sure to provide a standard lamp as well. Flourescent fixtures, such as Vita-Lite bulbs, are excellent for this purpose.

Wherever possible, suspend the lamps so they are above and outside the terrarium. If this is not possible, build a wire cage to fit securely around the bulb and fixture. Do not provide a lamp that lizards may actually touch! Be sure to keep a smoke detector in rooms with reptile units. While fires from properly set up terraria are rare, taking precautions is always important.

Monitors must have lighting during the daytime. It is generally easiest to put all lights on timers (available at most drug and hardware stores) with a twelve-hour day/night cycle. During cooler months, you may wish to change this to eight hours of light and sixteen hours of dark. Some breeders believe that such cyclic changes later induce breeding when lizards are returned to the twelve-hour cycle, but there is still too little evidence available to make this claim (for monitors) with much confidence.

The question of what substrate to use is common and often yields surprisingly heated discussion. I prefer a bare-floor terrarium, with the floor made of solid wood, concrete, or glass. Any loose substrate material, such as sand, soil, or wood chips (cork bark is okay, but cedar is deadly toxic) will be shifted by the lizards to produce what humans would consider a mess. One of the aesthetic problems with loose substrates is that they will be moved by the lizards, destroying whatever look they were intended to provide. All monitors dig, so plowing through substrate is the rule. I have used matting moss as a substrate for small monitors of the climbing variety with some success. Many loose substrates, such as gravel and corncob, can pose a danger because they can be accidentally swallowed by lizards and cause lethal internal impactions. It is also a difficult task to clean a cage with loose substrate.

Alternately, newspaper, paper towels, and brown butcher paper make effective substrate materials that are analogous to paper at the bottom of a birdcage. They are easy to place and remove (after getting the lizards out of the enclosure), and they generally can contain all the trash that must be periodically removed. They are also cheap materials that are readily available. For the standard glass terrarium, these are the substrates that will give you the least amount of difficulty.

There has also been the recent introduction of calcium-based terrarium "sand," which can be purchased at many pet shops. This material is nontoxic, is possibly of some nutrient value, and comes in a variety of colors. I use this material with success for varanids in smaller terraria (20–50 gallon) when aesthetics are important.

Large bark chips are not a substrate of choice, as they may cause irritation around the bases of the lizard's claws and cause

Savannah monitors will climb, especially if it gets them nearer to a heat source. Photo taken at the Alexander Koenig Museum in Bonn.

infection. Smaller grade bark such as orchid (fir) bark is less of a health problem but produces considerable dust that is not necessarily going to stay in the terrarium. In general, go with the simplest solution from the standpoint of the size of your lizard and ease of keeping the enclosure clean.

Though varanids frequent the tropics, this does not equate with meteorologically static environments of constant intense heat. Though grassland monitors may face warm season daytime high temperatures of 105° Fahrenheit (F) or more, most thrive in the range of 85–98° F. Nighttime lows may approach 72° F during the warm season. As temperatures rise, lizards become less active, either retreating to cover for the period of midday intensity, or going into an inactive period of estivation for several weeks to two to three months.

Alternately, the cooler season may have daytime highs in the 78–90° F range, with evening temperatures dropping to about 44° F. If temperatures stay in the low numbers, lizards may again go into a prolonged dormant state. Most ecological evidence suggests that both daily and seasonal temperature fluctuations are important for a variety of hormonal and behavioral (which are largely hormone controlled) responses and activities.

The best vivaria offer lizards a thermal gradient. This means that one end of the cage will be heated to its maximum temperature—say 95° F—but the other end will offer a much cooler

The emerald monitor, *V. prasinus,* represents what is arguably the greatest display of bright coloring in a living varanid. These graceful tree-dwellers are found in New Guinea.

region. Cooler may mean 80° F, but it should be enough that lizards can escape the threat of overheating. Put basking sites in the hot end of the cage, and hiding places in the cool. The idea of a thermal gradient is that it allows the lizard to select the temperature at which it is comfortable while also making it possible to adjust that temperature by moving from one place to another (known as thermal shuttling, a form of behavioral thermoregulation).

People frequently ask about cage mates for their monitors. Again, there are no hard and fast rules, except that monitors should not be housed with lizards much different in size from themselves. I have seen many mixed exhibit cages with monitors and water dragons (*Physignathus* sp.), prehensile-tailed skinks (*Corucia* sp.), and green iguanas (*Iguana* sp.), with all residents living in apparent harmony. Alternately, I had a large monitor that consumed another lizard that was about two-thirds its size. The safe answer is to house only one species per enclosure. Do not crowd any single terrarium, but make sure there is ample room for each lizard, including basking, climbing, and hiding places.

Provide a variety of large rocks for larger varanids, so that the lizard's claws wear down. The benefit of a monitor with trim claws will not be lost on anyone who has been passively scratched by a fair-sized lizard. Try to avoid using soft woods, as claws may lodge and digits become damaged.

FEEDING AND NUTRITION

R eptile keepers generally hold that monitor lizards prefer food items that challenge the fullness of their gape. In fact, field and museum studies on the diet of savannah monitors provide evidence that they favor a diet made predominantly of invertebrates, including millipedes, centipedes, scorpions, large insects, and the odd small lizard or snake. Eggs are also readily accepted as food.

Cape monitors, which are much larger than savannah monitors as adults, will consume the aforementioned foods, but also consume small birds and mammals, and larger snakes, including venomous species. Similar accounts of taking venomous snake prey have been relayed for Bengal and Indian monitors. It is neither necessary nor recommended that captive monitors be offered such foods in captivity, for reasons of practicality and safety.

Virtually all medium to large monitors will consume carrion. Wild monitors have readily consumed the putrefying remains of most vertebrates, from fishes to pheasants to buffaloes. Given that many populations may make carrion a staple of their diet, it is interesting to note the reluctance many herpetoculturists have to feeding raw meat or eggs to captive lizards. The concern, of course, is possible infection by the bacterium *Salmonella*. The symptoms and outcome of salmanellosis are serious and unpleasant to lizard and human, and may lead to fatality. I can point out that many keepers, myself included, have offered raw beef, chicken, lamb, eggs, and fish to monitors for decades without encountering a salmonella incident. Foods offered are always fresh (not putrefying) and either eaten or removed within a few hours of being offered. Containers that were in contact with such foods, including dishes and cage floors, are cleaned shortly after feeding, and substrates completely removed and washed (if Astroturf) or changed.

The Philippine "butuaan" is the only monitor known to feed specifically—but not exclusively—on fruits in the wild. It is also known as Gray's monitor, *V. olivaceus.*

All grassland monitors—savannah, Cape, Argus, Bengal, and Indian—will accept a wide variety of foods. Though variety itself is a factor debated by many herpeticulturists (i.e., is it necessary to provide a highly varied, slightly varied, or uniform diet?), there is no doubt that variety is not harmful. Furthermore, I subscribe to the idea that almost any animal may become bored with a steady diet of only one foodstuff. For this reason it may be prudent to offer caged varanids a regular supply of a staple prey items, such as large insects, supplemented by whatever additional food items become available. My preference for feeding monitors beef stems from the fact that even lean butcher-shop beef can be purchased at a far lower cost per pound than live rodents cost and does not involve the smell associated with mice and rats. Granted, the variety of prey items available through most commercial sources is generally limited to crickets, king worms, and rodents, but several brands of canned foods are available for reptiles. I have also used several brands of canned dog foods, available at a very reasonable price at most grocery stores. Monitors will generally feed on canned foods, but troublesome eaters may need food to be scented with something more familiar. I've added dead crickets or pieces of mouse hair to such foods to prompt lizards to take nonmoving food.

To the disbelief of many herpetoculturists, many monitors will consume fruits and vegetables. Though such observations are usually limited to Asian species, such as *V. olivaceus, V. prasinus,* and *V. beccarii,* captive savannah monitors have been observed to take vegetable matter on a regular basis. I have seen one longtime captive in the care of Barry and Pat Pomfret in England, who would share greens with iguanas feeding from a common bowl. Other savannah and white-throat monitors I have seen have readily taken fruits and cooked pasta. All these specimens were also routinely fed mice, canned dog food, or other meat products, but the tendency to take vegetable foods may be indicative that these lizards are more versatile in habits than we predicted. Given the highly irregular availability of foods in savannah habitats, such broad tastes may be an essential element in surviving in the wild state.

Hatchling monitors should be fed a diet of insects that are coated and fed reptile vitamin and mineral supplements that include vitamin D_3. Calcium supplementation is also necessary in young lizards (alternate feedings). As soon as the young can handle larger foods, offer goldfish, pink or fuzzy mice, and small pieces of beef or ground turkey. Continue to add supplements to all foods for young lizards. Older lizards eat less frequently, but also require supplementation. However, adults should be used to a more varied diet, supplementation may be less frequent than that offered hatchlings.

Much has been written about diets for carnivorous lizards, most based on successful maintenance of species over a long time period (i.e., Sprackland, 1995). However, far less has been documented about the actual dietary needs of the animals. For example, humans require UV light in order to synthesize the active form of vitamin D, and the literature frequently claims

that reptiles have this same need. Yet I have been unable to find experimental evidence in print to confirm this. Captive varanids may live and thrive for years without exposure to UV-B lights. We do know that diurnal lizards that have a parietal eye, including all varanids, do use UV light to regulate activity and gauge photoperiod, features that in turn regulate hormone utilization, activity, and many behaviors. The literature is clear that lizards given full-spectrum lighting tend to be much healthier, grow faster, and live longer than those without such lighting. My point is to observe your lizards and weigh all claims carefully. What we do not know about reptile physiology is still far more than what we do know.

Having said that, should you use vitamin and mineral supplements in foods for your monitors? Probably. Gut loading crickets with such compounds provides nutritious meals. Gut loading is giving prey species—usually crickets and king-worms—several feedings of leafy vegetables sprinkled with vitamin and mineral supplements. The concept that you are what you eat means, in this case, a cricket fed a decent diet is more nutritionally valuable to your lizard than one fed old newspapers and cricket droppings.

Calcium requirements for captive reptiles are well documented, as captive diets seem to be nutrient low and fat high (just like our own diets!). I add supplements to lizard foods as a regular aspect of feeding. Calcium is added to every feeding (or three times per week) and vitamins about every fourth feeding.

Juveniles should be offered food daily. As lizards reach a subadult stage, they may take less food, perhaps four times per week. Monitors over 20 inches may safely be fed twice weekly, and those over 28 inches do fine if offered regular weekly feedings. True giants over 4 feet in length may feed every two to three weeks if offered two to three rats or the equivalent. Unlike snakes, though, lizards generally feed frequently. If you try to treat a monitor like a snake and feed it only once a month, expect it to slowly languish and die.

Monitors tend to be hungrier and digest faster when hot than they are during a cooling period. If animals have become dormant during the cooling phase of a thermal cycling, expect them to be ravenous during the initial days of the hot phase and feed them accordingly.

Different species of monitors may have drastically different temperaments. Argus monitors will virtually pounce on food as soon as they see it, and you may need to separate specimens during feeding. Savannah and white-throat monitors are generally less aggressive, but be sure to watch animals during feeding to be sure each lizard gets adequate food. As a rule of thumb, "adequate food" may be thought of as a portion about the size of the body (between the axillae and the groin) of the monitor.

HANDLING

Many monitors make tractable, peaceful "pets," and no doubt the ability to handle a small "dragon" is part of the allure of these species as captives. Nevertheless, the size and general natural disposition of monitors means they must always be handled with caution and with proper precautions.

Even a passive monitor doing little more than perching on your arm or shoulder may rip skin and cause bleeding if the lizard's claws are sharp. Varanids typically have very sharp claws that can be used to eviscerate wild prey. To circumvent unwanted scratches, allow lizards to have large flat rocks in the terrarium to wear down the sharp tips of claws. Nail clippers that are sold for large cage birds may also be used, but be sure to get initial advice from someone who has manicured monitors. A simple added precaution is to handle larger monitors with gloves and wear long sleeves.

All savannah-dwelling monitors have a defensive reaction that may injure their human keeper. Monitors may coil and quickly lash their tails as whips. The scaled, muscular structure is unlikely to break bones (a commonly heard story), but even a 25-inch monitor can raise a painful welt on bare flesh. Getting

This welt was caused by the tail lash of a large monitor.

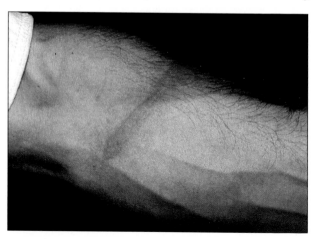

All large monitors can inflict serious lacerations with their sharp claws. Regular claw trimming is necessary if you intend to handle these species.

whipped in the eye is a serious injury. Tail whipping is especially likely when monitors are carried from above—that is, with your hands around their nape and over the hips, leaving the tail quite free. Experienced handlers often brace the tail under the arm that is also carrying the hips.

Tame and smaller monitors may be handled safely by placing them on top of your forearm, their shoulders securely grasped by your hand from below, the tail under your supporting arm. Animals over 3 feet, though, should be handled in a more secure manner. Grasp the lizard from above, holding the neck and the front of the shoulders. The other hand should grab over the hips, and the tail goes under that arm. Be careful of claws, as they could flail and may cause deep scratches that are easily infected. Do not handle large monitors (4 feet or more) unless you have another person helping.

If you are bitten, do not jerk or pull to get away. Remember that monitor teeth are recurved, so you only make the injury worse if you pull. In many cases you may need to wait for the lizard to let go. In more persistent cases, immerse the lizard in water. Though most monitors can remain submerged for a considerable time, those immersed in this manner often release quickly.

Bites should be taken seriously, especially if given by a large lizard. The possibility of you getting an infection is not to be underestimated, so see your physician as soon as feasible. Bites from larger lizards may require stitches.

BREEDING

Breeding reptiles in captivity has become the grail of modern herpetoculture. Captive-bred progeny are free of scars, missing digits, and other defects inflicted upon wild-caught lizards. They have fewer parasites and less adjustment to make to captive conditions. The argument that captive-hatched monitors will reduce the number of wild-collected ones so far remains just an argument. The number of imported lizards, particularly from Africa, is considerable and probably two orders of magnitude beyond contemporary breeding output. The fact that the cost of importing baby African monitors is still so low may delay large-scale commercial breeding efforts in the U.S. and Europe.

Among the savannah dwelling species, all have been bred in captivity, though only the Argus monitor is being bred with any regularity. Though few accounts have been published on breeding the Argus monitor, there is considerable word-of-mouth data available, along with the promising revelation that the breeding process is relatively simple to induce. With a few variations, the information given here applies to breeding most monitors in captivity.

Savannah monitors have been imported in gravid (egg-bearing) condition when as small as 18 inches (about two years old). Keepers report that captive-hatched specimens fed well in captivity may reach sexual maturity in twelve to eighteen months, but it is generally safe to assume that lizards will be of breeding age after the age of two years.

Though having roomy facilities is a plus when planning to breed monitors, these lizards have been known to make due in fairly compact enclosures. My friend Andy Rowell must rank among the first to breed savannah monitors in captivity, doing this with facilities restricted to one small room in his home in central England.

Begin by keeping the sexes in separate vivaria, preferably

only one lizard per enclosure. After a period in captivity that allows you to be sure of the overall health of the animals, begin introducing a cool cycle with shorter daylight periods. The cooling period may last one to three months. During this time, reduce the food offered to the lizards—some individuals may stop feeding altogether at this time.

Allow the cooling cycle to be determined by your local environment. Reducing the heat from December through March is in accord with outdoor conditions in North America (and may benefit your utilities bill, too).

Next, increase both photoperiod and heat gradually over a three-to-four-week period until you provide hot season temperatures. Feed lizards as much as possible on a daily or an alternate day basis. After lizards have put on some bulk, introduce the female into the male's vivarium. When a male intends mating, his behavior may appear belligerent to a human observer. He may hiss, claw, and grapple with the female. Eventually, if she is willing to mate, the lizards begin copulation, which may take a few minutes to over an hour. Mating may be repeated immediately or a day or two later; generally it is best to remove the female within a day of mating.

Continue feeding the lizards, and be especially sure that the female is getting a diet rich (not overloaded) with calcium. If you have been offering other foods, this is a good time to provide small mice or lizards, as well as meats with calcium added. Watch the female carefully over the next few weeks, as her increased bulk should be derived from both food and forming eggs.

Provide a nest box of moist (not wet) sand and vermiculite or moss. The box may be a simple plastic shoebox or an elaborate birdhouse structure, but it should have a substrate that will appeal to a lizard looking to lay eggs.

When the eggs are laid, remove them as soon as possible (monitors may eat their own eggs, or walk over them). Eggs may be laid all at one time or over several days, so check the nest box frequently. Move the eggs to an incubator that contains a compound of vermiculite and water mixed 50:50 by weight. Some breeders suggest a 5 part vermiculite to 4 part water compound; experiment and see what works best for you. Eggs should be one-half to two-thirds buried in the vermi-

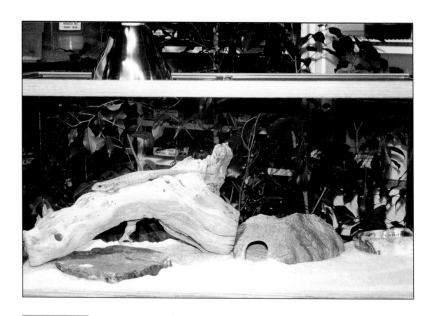

culite. The incubator can be a commercially available unit (these cost $50–$500, depending on your needs) or a simpler homemade unit. Many keepers place four to five eggs into a gallon jar with the vermiculite substrate. The lid keeps humidity high, and is removed periodically (weekly) to allow some fresh air into the incubator. Incubate eggs in a warm, dark place (such as a linen closet) at a temperature of 78–88° F. Do not turn lizard eggs while they incubate, as this may kill embryos. Be sure to calibrate the incubator to be sure of temperature before adding eggs, and give the device at least twenty-four hours in which to stabilize at the test temperature.

If all goes well, eggs will hatch after several months. Argus monitors hatch in four to six months, while savannah and white-throat monitors may take four to seven months. Bengal monitor eggs hatch in six to nine months, thus showing considerable variation in incubation time. Whether this variation is a factor of the mother's age, her diet, ambient incubation temperature, or humidity is unknown and worthy of further inquiry.

Some reptiles, including turtles and crocodilians, have the sex of offspring determined by the temperature of incubation (thermally induced sex). But monitors have chromosomal sex determination, like we do. However, while human males are the heterogametic sex (having one X and one Y chromosome), in monitors it is just the opposite (called the ZW system). Thus, a male monitor is ZZ and a female is ZW.

Once the lizards begin to hatch, avoid the urge to help them out of their eggs. The process of slitting an egg and fully emerging may take a few hours or two days. When the newly hatched lizards (called neonates) emerge, they will be moist and may still bear a small portion of the yolk sac on their belly. This will be lost within a few days and the large umbilical slit will close completely. Lizards are unlikely to feed while still carrying a yolk sac; in fact, most small lizards do not accept insect food for the first several days after hatching. Remember that egg yolk has an extremely high fat content, which stores well and provides a slow-burning energy supply. If neonates don't feed for the first week it is often because they don't need to eat yet.

Neonates of all the grassland monitors are large by the standards of most lizards, which spares you the need to find difficult-to-obtain foods such as fruit flies. Even a small savannah monitor (4 inches total length) can take mealworms for its first feeding. They can also take medium and large crickets, though it may take a few days for them to learn to compensate for the speed of such prey. The other species can take similar foods, though young Indian, Bengal, and white-throat monitors will be able to consume pink mice. As soon as the lizards are feeding reliably (about three weeks of regularly accepting food), I would recommend adding nonlive prey to their diets. This not only broadens their nutrient sources, but makes it easier for you to provide bulk to their diets.

While grassland monitors are babies they can safely be housed together. It is best not to overcrowd them, though, as some will be less able to obtain food or a desirable basking site. If housed in a 30-gallon terrarium (roughly 30 inches x 12 inches) you should house no more than six neonates. By the time the lizards reach a total length of 10 inches or start to attack each other, separate them into individual terraria, or at least house them in pairs. Young lizards should be alert and active, and thus require food daily. If properly fed and housed, young monitors should more than double in size their first year.

VETERINARY CONCERNS

Once you get your exotic lizards you should inquire as to the whereabouts of a qualified veterinarian who is familiar with herpetological medicine. This can take some work on your part, because most vets are not experienced in such matters, and reptile physiology is very different from that of a dog or horse. Among other concerns are the slower response time to drugs, calculating proper dosages, and recognizing reptile-specific diseases. If you wait to find a vet until you need one, you may be too late to save your lizard.

The simplest way to find a qualified herpetologically oriented veterinarian is to ask potential vets if they are members of the Association of Reptile and Amphibian Veterinarians (ARAV). You may also consult the ARAV Web site at www.arav.org or ask someone at the local zoo or herpetological society for a referral.

With the plethora of detailed books on reptile medicine available today, it is tempting to diagnose and treat your animal without seeing a vet. After all, vets cost money and so do prescription drugs. Your choice will in large part be based on how much you value your animal. If you sincerely care about your animal, take it to the vet! What you get for expensive office visits are six years of veterinary training, years of experience in diagnosing and treating diseases, the ability to prescribe appropriate drugs or therapies, resources that you don't have at home (such as blood and fecal testing), plus peace of mind that comes from dealing with a professional healer. It is all too easy to self-treat an animal with some old antibiotics, see it get well, then fail to connect its death several months later because of overdose poisoning (renal failure is a fairly common result of inappropriate drug therapy, but it may not manifest until several months after the drug was administered). Vets are trained to anticipate such problems. No, I am not a vet, and no the vets don't give me a percentage of customer income. But I have kept reptiles for four decades, and I know the value of professional advice in any field. I don't fix my own car, rebuild my computer, or diagnose my own illnesses. And when I have a sick lizard (or dog), we go to the vet. Period.

That said, you could still be of help to your vet because you know your animal better than anyone else does. Prepare by asking yourself the following questions before going to the vet. Has the lizard been feeding regularly? Does it eat all the food you offer? Are its feces loose or solid? Is the animal lethargic? Does it sleep a lot more than usual? Are you handling it more/less lately? In fact, it wouldn't hurt to keep a checklist of certain factors in your lizard's life that can be used to collect baseline health information. Among the additional items to include would be:

- Daytime temperature high/low in cage
- Nighttime temperature
- If water is taken regularly
- Types and frequency of feedings
- Date of last shed
- If animal is caged alone; if not, note when cage mate was added

You should be aware of some fairly obvious signs of disease. Of course, any departure from normal behavior is a clue that something may be wrong, but certain symptoms are much more diagnostic than others. Typical reptilian signs that something is amiss include loss of appetite, lethargy, staying hidden, gasping or gaping, and wheezing. Any lizard displaying one of these symptoms should be isolated from other lizards and housed alone in a quarantine terrarium.

For purposes of hygiene and observation, I recommend that quarantine enclosures be kept as simple as possible. I use plain glass aquaria with either newspaper or paper towel substrate, a disposable cardboard box (such as a shoebox) hide, and a large bowl for water. Such cages are stripped and cleaned daily.

Incidentally, if a veterinarian prescribes drug therapy, be sure to administer the full course of treatment. If you stop giving an antibiotic when symptoms disappear, residual bacteria may seriously reinfect the animal, become stronger, and become immune to further treatment by the same drug. Result:

you will have to start treatment from scratch with a new drug, and you may still lose the lizard.

Remember that veterinary medical treatment works first on alleviating symptoms of an illness. To prevent additional illnesses in your collection, or reinfection of a single animal, you must address the probable causes for the illness. In most cases, assuming you purchased a healthy animal in the first place, the cause of an illness is most commonly found in one of the following situations (in rough order of likelihood):

- Improper temperature regime
- Infection from a cage mate
- Unsanitary terrarium (includes use of toxic substrate, such as cedar)
- Undetected scratch (which leads to infection)
- Overcrowded terraria
- Improper diet

Following is a list of the most commonly encountered veterinary problems seen in monitors. I present these conditions in rough order of commonness, and suggest preliminary treatment where appropriate. This is far from a comprehensive listing, so do not consider symptoms not described here unimportant.

Mouth Rot

This is an insidious, common, infectious, and potentially lethal disease that goes by the technical name of stomatitis. Early symptoms include wheezing or gurgling sounds, tiny bubbles in the nostrils, and swelling of the lips. Examination of the mouth shows teeth and gums covered in a whitish, pasty substance. There are two main varieties of this disease, both contagious to other reptiles and both requiring prompt veterinary care. One form is treated primarily by antibiotic injection, the other by surgery and antibiotics. Once returned home, lizards should be kept in warm, dry terraria with clean drinking (not soaking) water. Be sure to change the water frequently. Keep ill lizards in quarantine, and wash hands thoroughly after handling animals or cage accessories. The terrarium should have a very warm (95–105° F) section and a cooler retreat area. Reptiles with bacterial infections often bask and induce fever to fight the disease, but still require an escape when temperatures threaten other physiological functions.

Remember that bacterial infections can be transmitted through infected water, so be sure to change cage water frequently during treatment period.

Temperature Stress

Lizards like it hot. Not warm, but hot. We may find an 80° F room warm and start the air conditioner, but to most monitors that same temperature is just shy of cool. Lizards need heat, usually in the range that we humans find uncomfortable. This is one good reason why reptiles should have their own room in a house.

Cold lizards fail to metabolize properly. They have neither energy to feed nor hormones telling them to hunt. Their immune systems become depressed, and their bodies begin slow catabolization, the process of breaking down to provide energy to stay alive. Increasing the heat in a terrarium is the first step to reviving cold-stressed lizards, but a diet-and-fluid-therapy regimen is also needed. These lizards may initially need to be force-fed. They may require water (or electrolyte-rich fluids such as Gatorade sports drink) from a dropper.

Alternately, you may provide too much heat, or a cage with the "right" temperature but no place to escape the heat. Heat-stressed lizards also require water and fluid-replacement therapy, but they may also be suffering more serious internal injury. Take such beasties to a vet for a complete examination.

Parasites

External parasites can often be discovered by closely examining your lizard. Small mites and ticks are commonly found in the nostrils, near the eyes, in armpits, near the cloaca, and in any skin folds. You can remove ticks with forceps, then treat the area with a topical application of an antibiotic ointment (such as Neosporin). Mites can be suffocated by dabbing them with olive or vegetable oil then removed by wiping with a paper towel an hour or two later.

The problem with external parasites lies more in keeping them away than in removing them from an animal. You must find and close the source of the parasites. More often than not, an owner did not sufficiently inspect a specimen on purchase or give it appropriate time in quarantine. Again, veterinarians have chemical treatments that should kill local parasites, and they can check infected lizards for secondary signs of parasite-induced stress.

Internal parasites are more difficult to detect. Some large intestinal worms may be apparent in feces, but to be safe and sure have fecal analyses performed on all newly acquired animals. While periodic subsequent examinations are not usually recommended, if you have particularly valuable lizards you may want to have annual exams conducted.

Respiratory Disease

Reptiles are subject to a variety of respiratory infections, including pneumonia and tuberculosis. The herpetological forms of these diseases are every bit as serious as their human counterparts. Proper diagnosis of the illness requires a veterinary examination.

Typical early symptoms of respiratory distress include loss or reduction of appetite, listlessness, and bubbling or gurgling sounds as the lizard breathes. In severe cases, bubbles may protrude from the nostrils (and are often accompanied by stomatitis, or mouth rot). If symptoms are detected early enough, a proper antibiotic treatment may effect a cure. Additional treatment is similar to that advised under stomatitis: increase the temperature and change drinking water frequently.

Gastrointestinal Blockage (Constipation)

Monitors are not spared the occasional problem of becoming blocked. There are numerous causes, including a restricted or inappropriate diet, insufficient heat, insufficient water, and disease. In many cases, this is a condition you should attempt to alleviate before consulting a veterinarian, barring any additional symptoms.

Increase the amount of water available to the animal and, if necessary, offer it water by catheter or dropper. A brief soaking in warm water may help initiate a fecal movement. Finally, adding a small amount of vegetable or olive oil to the lizard's diet may move things along. If these treatments fail to produce a substantial fecal movement within forty-eight hours, I suggest you have your vet examine the lizard.

Some authors claim that blockage caused by excessive hair collected in the gut may be treated by giving lizards additional drinking water. While this may facilitate movement in minor cases, more severe cases will not respond. This is because hair does not dissolve in water. For such cases, take the animal to a veterinarian who can treat the condition safely and effectively.

Bites and Wounds

Monitors are predators and as such have sharp claws and teeth. Animals may bite each other when seizing the same food item, when mating, or by accident. Claws may passively open skin when one lizard walks across another. Sharp objects in cages may cut the lizards, and live rodents are common causes of severe cuts and bites.

Infections thrive in warm temperatures (recall that even small cuts are considered more serious in the tropics), so treatment should be swift. Establish the cause of the cut and remove it—this may require separation of lizards into individual quarters. Wash the wound with warm water and, if possible, an antiseptic such as Betadine. Apply a topical antibiotic cream, such as Polysporin, and keep the lizard warm and dry until it heals.

At any sign of continued bleeding, or spreading infection, take the lizard to the veterinarian. Many infections require injection therapy.

LIFE STAGES

Part of the proper care of lizards requires the keeper to provide for the age and condition of the charges. We have all been exposed to dog food commercials telling us how Fido needs different foods at different times. So do reptiles. De Vosjoli, Donoghue and Klingenberg (1999) have proposed a life stages model worth studying by anyone serious about herpetoculture. The five-stage version consists of:

1) **Prebirth/Embryonic:** This stage is spent within the confines of the egg. It is affected by incubation conditions including temperature and substrate moisture. Other factors that may affect embryo health include the diet and health of the mother and the genetics of both parents.

2) **Hatchling/Juvenile Stage:** This stage is characterized by small size, high propensity for flight or defensive behaviors, rapid growth, and high feeding rate. Shedding rates are high. Feeding is the primary drive of this stage.

3) **Sexual Onset/Adolescence:** This stage is characterized by the onset of sexual and competitive behaviors. Seasonal patterns of sexual behavior will become apparent as will agonistic behaviors, usually between males. Growth rate usually tapers. In captivity, some species of monitors that start off as aggressive become more docile by the time they reach this stage.

4) **Sexual Maturity:** As animals grow older, they continue to reproduce but after a few years enter a reproductive decline. Growth rate tapers drastically.

5) **Old Age:** Growth halts. Periods between sheds become longer. Reproductive rate declines and eventually stops. Activity levels are reduced. Diet must be adjusted to meet the needs of this stage, basically less food per week.

CONCLUSION

Herpetology is a wonderful branch of biology that focuses on what many people feel are the most fascinating animals on earth. By bringing reptiles into our homes and laboratories, the possibilities to learn about them and contribute to the larger science are increased. But there is a price if you want to contribute to science: you must publish.

Have you bred white-throat monitors? If so, you may only be interested in selling the young. But if you want to contribute to herpetology, you must publish your observations or you have effectively accomplished nothing. Good science involves sharing, which is why every biologist acknowledges people in every publication from short paper to massive treatise.

There are many routes to publication. Start with notes for your local herpetological society. Write to the editors of the herpetocultural magazines and request writer's guidelines. These will tell you how a professional manuscript should be assembled. Read everything you can find so you may imitate the format. Don't be afraid to write, but do your part by proofreading and editing before sending anything to an editor. Have friends read your manuscript. If there is something they do not understand, you should rewrite it.

Though many people have bred the monitors discussed in this book, there is precious little published, and many of my sources have been word of mouth. There is no need for such interesting and vital information to be unpublished and difficult to track down. If you make good observations and have success with your reptiles, publish the findings. That way we all learn and benefit from your experience.

If your study of reptiles is serious, you will no doubt want to gain access to more literature and people who can share your interest. I have already suggested that you join your local herpetological society, giving you access to people you can meet with regularly to share your interests. Some of the regional societies, such as those in New York, Chicago, Philadelphia, and Maryland, are quite large, and represent an "intermediate" step between the local and large national organizations. Among the major organizations are those that publish the periodicals listed in the bibliography plus the International Herpetological Symposium. The latter is not a society but a consortium that hosts annual meetings where the focus is on herpetoculture.

To find journals and addresses for societies, you should obtain access to a good natural history library, such as that at a museum or university. Many of these organizations, as well as the herpetological societies, have Web sites, so access may be a few mouse clicks away. There are also numerous herpetological Web sites, and there is often interesting information available. But beware of some site information—it is not edited or subject to any review, so it is possible to find (as I do) frequent errors. Perhaps in a few years the quality will improve, but for now check your sources carefully.

About the Author

Robert George Sprackland, Ph.D., has kept reptiles and amphibians since 1964. His interests focus on evolution, behavior, ecology, and herpetoculture. He was a cofounder of the Kansas Herpetological Society and is an elected Fellow of the Linnean and Zoological Societies of London. His other books include the popular *All About Lizards, Giant Lizards,* and *Aquaterrariums* (1995), and he is a regular contributor to *Reptiles* magazine. He studied herpetology and paleontology at the University of Kansas (BA), San Jose State University (MA) and University College London (Ph.D.), where he conducted the bulk of his research at the Natural History Museum, London. He is a world-recognized authority on monitor lizards, having spent thirty years studying these lizards. Robert is the Director of the Virtual Museum of Natural History at curator.org, a nonprofit online scientific and educational organization.

RESOURCES

I n addition to the specific books and articles listed below, you are advised to subscribe to one or more of the magazines now available on herpetoculture. These provide insights and experiences from novice and seasoned reptile keepers, and often provide new methods for better keeping your animals.

The major U.S. periodicals are:

Herpetological Natural History
c/o David Hulmes
361 Van Winkle Avenue
Hawthorne, NJ 07506

Herpetological Review
c/o Robert Aldridge
Dept. of Biology
Saint Louis University
3507 Laclede Avenue
St. Louis, MO 63103-2010

Reptiles Magazine
P.O. Box 58700
Boulder, CO 80323-8700
www.reptilesmagazine.com
(800) 361-4132

Works Cited

I have restricted my references to publications in English unless they were specifically mentioned in the text.

Alberts, Allison. 1994. Off to see the lizard: lessons from the wild. *The Vivarium* 5 (5):26–28.

Anderson, John. 1989. Zoology of Egypt. Volume first. *Reptilia and batrachia*. London: Bernard Quaritch.

Auffenberg, Walter. 1981. *The Behavioral Ecology of the Komodo monitor*. Gainesville: University of Florida Presses.

Auffenberg, Walter. 1994. *The Bengal Monitor*. Gainesville: University of Florida Presses.

Balsai, Michael. 1997. *General Care and Maintenance of Popular Monitors and Tegus.* Advanced Vivarium Systems.

Balsai, Michael. 1992. *The General Care and Maintenance of Savannah Monitors and Other Popular Monitor Species.* Advanced Vivarium Systems.

Bartlett, R. D., and P. Bartlett. 1996. *Monitors, Tegus, and Related Lizards.* Hauppauge, N.Y.: Barron's.

Bayless, Mark, and Tim Reynolds. 1992. Breeding of the savannah monitor lizard in captivity (*Varanus exanthematicus Bosc*, 1792). *Herpetology (Southwestern Herpetological Society)* 22 (1):12–14.

Bayless, Mark, and Robert Sprackland. 2000. The taxonomy of Africa's savanna and Cape monitor lizards. Parts 1 and 2. *Reptiles* 8 (6); 8 (7).

Bennett, Daniel. 1998. *Monitor Lizards: Natural History, Biology and Husbandry.* Frankfurt: Edition Chimaira.

Berg, Doug. 1987. The savannah monitor *(Varanus exanthematicus). Northern California Herpetological Society Newsletter* 6 (1):6.

Bernard, Susan. 1996. *The Reptile Keeper's Handbook.* Malabar, Fla.: Krieger Publishing.

Böhme, Wolfgang. 1989. Zur Genitalmorphologie der Sauria: funktionelle und Stammesgeschichtliche Aspekte. *Bonner Zoologische Monographien* 27:1–176.

Böhme, Wolfgang & Thomas Ziegler. 1997. A taxonomic review of the Varanus *(Polydaedalus) niloticus* (Linnaeus, 1766) complex. *Herpetological Journal* 7:155–162.

Branch, Bill. 1982. Hemipeneal morphology of the platynotan lizards. *Journal of Herpetology* 16:16–38.

Caldwell, Michael. 1999. Squamate phylogeny and the relationships of snakes and mosasaurids. *Zoological Journal of the Linnean Society* 125 (1):115–147.

De Vosjoli, Philippe. 1999. Guidelines for the responsible keeping of large reptiles, Part 2: guidelines for regulation. *The Vivarium* 10 (3):41–42.

De Vosjoli,P., Donoghue, S., and R. Klingenberg. 1999. The Interactive Multifactorial Model of Herpetoculture: Part 1: Introduction and Ontogeny. *The Vivarium* 11 (1):30–37.

Eidenmüller, Bernd. 1998. *Warane: Lebensweise, Pflege, Zucht.* Offenbach Germany: Herpeton.

Holmes, R. S., M. King, and D. King. 1975. Phenetic relationships among varanid lizards based upon comparative electrophoretic data and karyotypic analysis. *Biochemical Systematics and Ecology* 3: 257–262.

James, C., J. Losos, and D. King. 1992. Reproductive biology and diets of goannas (Reptilia: Varanidae) from Australia. *Journal of Herpetology* 26:128–136.

King, Dennis & Brian Green. 1999. *Goanna: The biology of varanid lizards, Second edition.* University of New South Wales Press, Sydney.

King, Max & Dennis King. 1975. Chromosomal evolution in the lizard genus *Varanus* (Reptilia). *Australian Journal of Biological Science* 28:89–108.

Lemm, Jeff. 1998. The natural history and captive husbandry of the white-throated monitor *(Varanus albigularis). Reptiles* 6 (2):10–21.

Losos, Jonathan, and Harry Greene. 1988. Ecological and evolutionary implications of diet in monitor lizards. *Biological Journal of the Linnean Society* 35:379–407.

Pfeiffer, P. 1964. *Aux Iles du Dragons.* Paris: Flammarion.

Phillips, John, and Robert Millar. 1998. Reproductive biology of the white-throated savanna monitor, *Varanus albigularis. Journal of Herpetology* 32 (3):366–377.

Phillips, John, and G. Packard. 1994. Influence of temperature and moisture on eggs and embryos of the white-throated savanna monitor, *Varanus albigularis:* Implications for conservation. *Biological Conservation* 69:131–136.

Pope, Clifford. 1955. *The Reptile World.* New York: Knopff.

Pregill, G., J. Gauthier, and H. Greene. 1986. The evolution of helodermatid squamates, with description of a new taxon and an overview of Varanoidea. *Transactions of the San Diego Natural History Society* 21:167–202.

Schmidt, Karl. 1919. Contributions to the herpetology of the Belgian Congo based on the collection of the American Museum Expedition 1909–1915. *Bulletin of the American Museum of Natural History* 39:385–624.

Schmidt, Karl, and Robert Inger. 1957. *Living Reptiles of the World.* New York: Doubleday.

Shine, Richard. 1986. Food habits, habitats and reproductive biology of four sympatric species of varanid lizards in tropical Australia. *Herpetologica* 42:346–360.

Sprackland, Robert. 1982. Feeding and nutrition of monitor lizards in captivity and in the wild. *Bulletin of the Kansas Herpetological Society* 47: 15–18.

Sprackland, Robert. 1990. A preliminary study of food discrimination in monitor lizards *(Reptilia: Lacertilia: Varanidae). Bulletin of the Chicago Herpetological Society* 25 (10):181–183.

Sprackland, Robert. 1991. The origin and zoogeography of monitor lizards of the subgenus *Odatria* Gray (Sauria: Varanidae): a re-evaluation. *Mertensiella* 2:240–252.

Sprackland, Robert. 1992. *Giant Lizards.* Neptune, New Jersey: T.F.H Publications.

Sprackland, Robert. 1995. Carnivorous lizards and their diet. *The Vivarium* 5 (5):12–14.

Strimple, Peter. 1988–1989. The savannah monitor *Varanus exanthematicus.* Parts 1–4; The Forked Tongue 13 (12):8–13; 14 (1):5–7; 14 (2):5–8; 14 (3):7–16.

Switak, Karl. 1998. Living in peril: Africa's savannah and white-throated monitors. *Reptiles* 6 (2):76–89.

Visser, Gerhardt. 1981. Breeding the white-throated monitor at Rotterdam Zoo. *International Zoo Yearbook* 21:87–91.

Web Sites

Association of Reptile and Amphibian Veterinarians: www.arav.org

National Reptile and Amphibian Advisory Council: www.nraac.org

The Virtual Museum of Natural History: curator.org

INDEX

African species, 22–30
aggression, 51
American species, 11
anatomy, 10–12
Argus monitor, 16, 30–33, 42–43
Asian species, 30–36, 49

behavior, 11, 35, 44, 51–52, 55
Bengal monitors, 30, 33, 47
bites to humans, 18–19, 53
bites/wounds, 63
black-throat monitor, 25
blue-tongue skinks, 15
Borneo species, 11
Bosc's monitor, 22
breeding, 54–57, 65. See also captive-bred
   specimens

cage mates, 46, 57
cages. See enclosures
Cape monitors. See white-throat monitor
captive-bred specimens, 41, 54
captive breeding, 18, 30, 34
choosing a monitor, 14, 37–40
claws, 46, 52
coloration: Argus monitors, 31; habitat
   and rainfall, 29; Indian monitors,
   34–35; variations in, 12
crocodile monitors, 15

dangers/hazards, 44, 46, 63
dealers, 39
desert monitors, 33
diet/nutrition: "adequate food," 51;
   African savannah monitors, 24–25;
   during breeding, 55; carnivorous nature
   of, 11; commercial foods, 48–49; at
   different life stages, 64; frequency of
   feeding, 17, 51; neonates, 56–57;
   prey foods, 48; supplements, 49–51
digestive system, 11–12
digging, 44
distinguishing features. See identifying
   features
diurnal lizards, 11
dorsal scales, 10, 28
Duméril's monitor, 18

earless "monitors" of Borneo, 11
egg-laying behavior, 11
enclosures, 40, 54–55
environment, 12–13, 22. See also
   enclosures; habitats
escaped pets, 15, 43
evolution of monitors, 9–10
eyes, 10, 11, 39

food. See diet/nutrition

gold monitors, 35

Gould's monitor species, 32, 33
grassland species, 13, 31, 57
Gray's monitor, 33

habitats: African savannahs, 27; loss of,
   19; of savannah monitors, 6;
   savannahs/grasslands, 12–13, 49.
   See also enclosures; range
habits. See behavior
handling, 15, 17, 52–53
health: bites/wounds, 63; causes of illness,
   60; collecting baseline information, 59;
   in choosing a monitor, 40; renal failure,
   58; Salmonella, 15, 47; temperature
   stress, 61; veterinary care, 40, 58.
   See also illness
heat sources, 43
hemipenal structure, 26
hissing, 11
husbandry, 16, 39–40. See also diet/
   nutrition; enclosures; health
hygiene, 17, 43, 47

illness: gastrointestinal blockage
   (constipation), 62–63; infections, 63;
   intestinal worms, 62; mites, 61; mouth
   rot, 60–61; parasites, 38, 40, 61–62;
   pneumonia, 15, 62; respiratory disease,
   62; symptoms, 38, 59. See also health
incubators, 56
Indian monitors, 33, 34, 47
Indian species, 30, 33, 57
infection, risk to humans, 15
intelligence, 13–14
interaction with humans, 13–14
international trade of lizards, 19

juveniles, 51

Komodo dragons, 12, 35–36

leather trade, 19, 24
legal issues, 18–19
length, 13–14, 24, 34
lethargy, 38
life expectancy, 15–16
life stages, 64
lighting, 43–44, 49–50.
   See also ultraviolet (UV)

metabolism, 61
mouth, healthy, 39

neonates, 56–57
nest boxes, 55
nests, 11
Nile monitors, 22–23
nostrils, 12, 26, 35, 39
nutrition. See diet/nutrition

obesity, 38. See also diet/nutrition
ocelli (eyelike spots), 28, 32
odor, 16
overheating, 46

parietal foramen, 11, 43
pet shops, 37–39

pets, monitors as, 13–19
pineal (or third) eye, 11
predatory nature, 13–14
prehensile-tailed skinks, 46
prehensile tails, 12

quarantine, 40, 59

range, 12, 26, 27, 29. See also habitats
responsibility of owners, 15, 17, 19, 3

safety, 52–53
Salmonella, 15, 47
savannah monitor (V. exanthematicu
   aggressiveness while feeding, 51;
   classification of, 21; size/temperam
   of African, 22–23;
savannah species: African, 24–25;
   captive-bred, 54; compared to whi
   throats, 26–27; diet/nutrition, 49;
   range of African, 23–24
scale structure, 10, 24, 28
seasonal feeding cycles, 51
sensory organs/processes, 10–11
sex determination, 56–57
species of varanids, numbers of, 12
stomatitis (mouth rot), 60–61

tails: Argus monitors, 32; defensive u
   52–53; monitors in general, 10, 12;
   white-throat monitors, 26
teeth, 39
temperament, 32, 51
temperature requirements, 43, 45, 56
terraria. See enclosures
thermal gradient, 43, 45–46
thermally induced sex, 56–57
thermoregulatory behavior, 11
third (or pineal) eye, 11
tongues, 11
tractability, 13–14
tree-climbing, 42–43
tree monitors, 24

ultraviolet (UV): light receptors, 11;
   UV-B light, 49–50

V. albigularis ionidesi, 26
V. bengalensis, 34
V. flavescens, 30
V. nebulosus, 33
V. olivaceus, 11
V. panoptes horni, 31
V. (Polydaedalus) exanthematicus, 21
V. priscus (or Megalania) (extinct), 1
veterinary care, 40, 58
vision, 10
vivaria. See enclosures

water requirements, 43, 63
white-throat monitor; aggressivenes
   while feeding, 51; compared to
   savannahs, 26–27; diet/nutrition, 4
   popularity of, 22–23, 25; range of,
   selling the young, 65
wild-caught specimens, 41
wounds, 63